ChrisNamesChrisNamesChrisNamesChrisNames

ChrisNamesChrisNamesChrisNamesChrisNamesChrisNamesChrisNamesChrisNames

ChrisNamesChrisNamesChrisNamesChrisNamesChrisNamesChrisNamesChrisNames

ChrisNames

ChrisNamesChrisNamesChrisNamesChrisNames

An Illustrated Guide to Chris Berman's Unique Characterizations of Sports Personalities

ChrisNames

BY CHRIS
"I'll Never Be Your Beast Of"
BERMAN

Illustrated by Dan Floersch

Edited by Louis Oppenheim

Andrews and McMeel
A Universal Press Syndicate Company
Kansas City

 For information write Andrews and McMeel, a Universal Press Syndicate Company, 4900 Main Street, Kansas City, Missouri 64112.

Designed by Barrie Maguire
Compiled by Matt Lombardi

Library of Congress Cataloging-in-Publication Data

Berman, Chris.
ChrisNames : an illustrated guide to Chris Berman's unique characterizations of sports personalities / by Chris "I'll Never Be Your Beast of" Berman ; illustrated by Dan Floersch.
p. cm.
ISBN 0-8362-1753-5 : $8.95
1. Athletes—Nicknames—United States. I. Title.
GV706.8.B47 1994
796—dc20 94-10756
CIP

CONTENTS

Nicknames by Category

1.
Going Places

Going Places in the U.S.A.

Daryl **Please Come to** Boston

What: Outfield
When: 1984-present
Where: Chicago White Sox, New York Mets, Colorado, New York Yankees
Why Should I Know This Guy?: Had hits in his first three major-league at bats

Jeff **Going Back to** Huson

What: Shortstop

When: 1988-present

Where: Montreal, Texas

Why Should I Know This Guy?:

Coming back from a broken left big toe in 1993

Dave **Death** Valle

What: Catcher

When: 1984-present

Where: Seattle, Boston

Why Should I Know This Guy?:

Hit by 17 pitches in 1993 to lead the American League

Mel **Carnegie** Hall

What: Outfield, DH

When: 1981-92

Where: Chicago Cubs, Cleveland, New York Yankees

Why Should I Know This Guy?:

Signed with the Lotte Marines of Japan after 1992 season

ChrisNamesChrisNamesChrisNamesChrisNames

HE FINDS IT EQUALLY
SUCCESSFUL GOING
TO THE ALLEYS...

©1993 FLOERSCH

FLO

ROBIN VENTURA
"HIGHWAY"

ChrisNamesChrisNamesChrisNamesChrisNames

Robin Ventura **Highway**

What: Third base

When: 1989-present

Where: Chicago White Sox

Why Should I Know This Guy?:

Apparently undamaged by Nolan Ryan's headlock

Jose **Costa** Mesa

What: Starting pitcher

When: 1987-present

Where: Baltimore, Cleveland

Why Should I Know This Guy?:

Led Indians staff with 10 wins in 1993

International

Bret Barberie **Coast**

What: Second base

When: 1991-present

Where: Montreal, Florida

Why Should I Know This Guy?:

Hit home runs from both sides of the plate in the same game, 1991

Mike **Nova** Scioscia

What: Catcher

When: 1980-present

Where: Los Angeles, San Diego, Texas

Why Should I Know This Guy?:

Led National League catchers in chances, 1987, 1989, 1990

Pat **North of the** Borders

What: Catcher

When: 1988-present

Where: Toronto

Why Should I Know This Guy?:

1992 World Series MVP; kept starting job in 1993 despite Toronto's phalanx of catching phenoms

Vicente **Buckingham** Palacios

What: Pitcher

When: 1987-present

Where: Pittsburgh, St. Louis

Why Should I Know This Guy?:

Threw only career shutout with Pirates in 1991

Brian **10** Downing **Street**

What: DH, outfield, catcher

When: 1973-92

Where: Chicago White Sox, California, Texas

Why Should I Know This Guy?:

Set the American League record for most consecutive errorless games by an outfielder – 244

Big Ben McDonald

What: Starting pitcher

When: 1989-present

Where: Baltimore

Why Should I Know This Guy?:

Held opposition in 1993 to a .228 batting average

2. Berman Goes Commercial

In the Medicine Cabinet

Dave Burba **Shave**

What: Pitcher
When: 1990-present
Where: Seattle, San Francisco
Why Should I Know This Guy?:
Hit for a .294 average in 1993, probably a result of having Bonds ahead of him in the lineup

ChrisNamesChrisNamesChrisNamesChrisNamesChrisNamesChrisNamesChrisNamesChrisNames
ChrisNamesChrisNamesChrisNamesChrisNamesChrisNamesChrisNamesChrisNamesChrisNames
ChrisNamesChrisNamesChrisNamesChrisNames

ChrisNamesChrisNamesChrisNamesChrisNames

ChrisNamesChrisNamesChrisNamesChrisNamesChrisNamesChrisNamesChrisNames

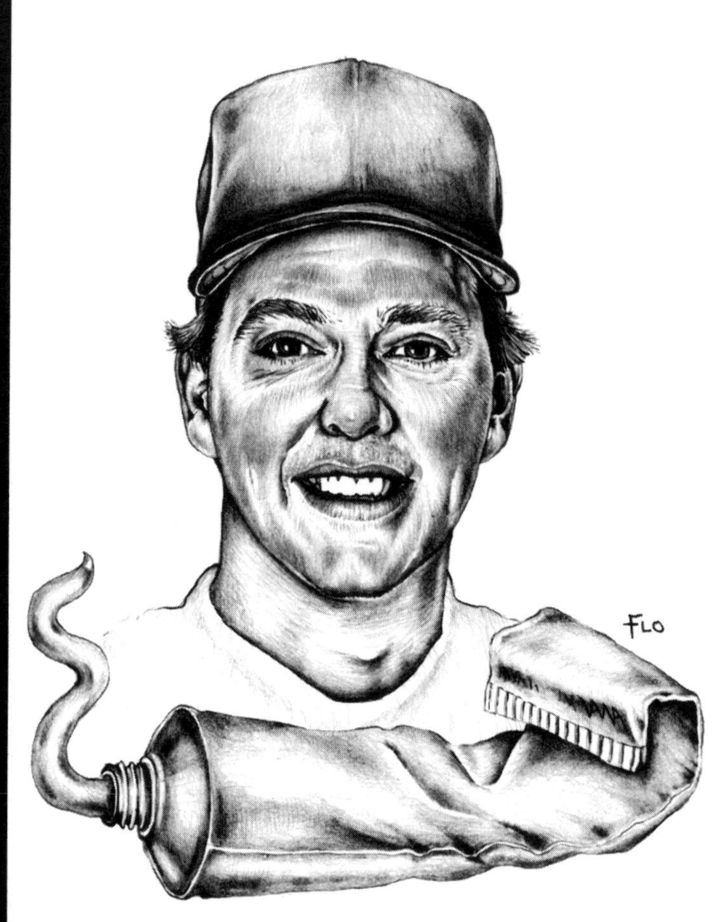

He knows how to execute the "squeeze."

WALLY "ABSORBINE" JOYNER

ChrisNamesChrisNamesChrisNamesChrisNamesChrisNamesChrisNamesChrisNames

ChrisNamesChrisNamesChrisNamesChrisNames

Kevin **Alka** Seitzer

What: Third base

When: 1986-present

Where: Kansas City, Oakland, Milwaukee

Why Should I Know This Guy?:

Led the American League in hits as a rookie; batting average declined each of the next four seasons

Pete **Raise Your Hand If You're** Schourek

What: Pitcher

When: 1991-present

Where: New York Mets, Cincinnati

Why Should I Know This Guy?:

Was used by the Mets as a pinch runner

Wally **Absorbine** Joyner

What: First base

When: 1986-present

Where: California, Kansas City

Why Should I Know This Guy?:

Was a rare write-in All-Star Game starter as a rookie

In the Kitchen

Dan **Man From** Gladden

What: Outfield

When: 1983-present

Where: San Francisco, Minnesota, Detroit

Why Should I Know This Guy?:
In a seven-game stint with Toledo in 1993, he hit .393; playing with the Tokyo Yomiuri Giants in 1994

Bill **Liquid** Plummer

What: Catcher; manager

When: 1968-78; 1992

Where: Chicago Cubs, Cincinnati, Seattle; Seattle

Why Should I Know This Guy?:
Was Johnny Bench's backup on Cincinnati's Big Red Machine dynasty of the '70s

On the Road

Todd **Mercedes** Benzinger

What: First base

When: 1987-present

Where: Boston, Cincinnati, Kansas City, Los Angeles, San Francisco

Why Should I Know This Guy?:
Led the National League with 628 at bats in 1989; has never been within 200 of that number before or since

Luis **Buick** Rivera

What: Middle infield

When: 1986-present

Where: Montreal, Boston, New York Mets

Why Should I Know This Guy?:
Set record for fewest errors by a shortstop who led his league in errors – 24, for Red Sox in 1991

Toys and Games

Scott **Milton** Bradley

What: Catcher

When: 1984-92

Where: New York Yankees, Chicago White Sox, Seattle, Cincinnati

Why Should I Know This Guy?: Traded by White Sox to Mariners in 1986 for a player to be named later—who turned out to be emerging star Ivan Calderon

Lance **Oh Darn, You Sunk My** Blankenship

What: Outfield, infield

When: 1988-present

Where: Oakland

Why Should I Know This Guy?: Another specimen from Tony La Russa's genetic engineering experiment to clone/replace Tony Phillips

Electronics

Tim Hulett **Packard**

What: Second base, third base

When: 1983-present

Where: Chicago White Sox, Baltimore

Why Should I Know This Guy?: Led American League third basemen in errors in 1985

Randy **Ever** Ready

What: Infield

When: 1983-present

Where: Milwaukee, San Diego, Philadelphia, Oakland, Montreal

Why Should I Know This Guy?: Was the Expos' choice to fill roster spot that opened when Delino DeShields was injured in 1993

JEFF MONTGOMERY

"WARD"

Department Stores

Jeff Montgomery **Ward**

What: Closer

When: 1987-present

Where: Cincinnati, Kansas City

Why Should I Know This Guy?:

Led the American League in saves, 1993 (or was that Duane **Montgomery** Ward?)

3. TV and Movies

Box Office Favorites

Neal **Body** Heaton

What: Pitcher

When: 1982-present

Where: Cleveland, Minnesota, Montreal, Pittsburgh, Kansas City, Milwaukee, New York Yankees

Why Should I Know This Guy?: Lost seventeen games as a starter for the Indians in 1985

Steve **Chariots of** Fireovid

What: Pitcher

When: 1981-92

Where: San Diego, Philadelphia, Chicago White Sox, Seattle, Texas

Why Should I Know This Guy?: Has pitched for 13 different minor-league teams

Edwin **High** Nunez

What: Relief pitcher

When: 1982-present

Where: Seattle, New York Mets, Detroit, Milwaukee, Texas, Oakland

Why Should I Know This Guy?: Began career as Mariners closer

Mike **Private** Benjamin

What: Infield

When: 1989-present

Where: San Francisco

Why Should I Know This Guy?: Born November 22, 1965 – second aniversary of the Kennedy assassination

It appears from here that he's doctoring the ball.

KEVIN "SPINAL"
TAPANI

Gary Sheffield **of Dreams**

What: Third base, outfield

When: 1988-present

Where: Milwaukee, San Diego, Florida

Why Should I Know This Guy?: Batting champion, 1992; seems to prefer playing near the ocean

Kevin **Spinal** Tapani

What: Starting pitcher

When: 1989-present

Where: New York Mets, Minnesota

Why Should I Know This Guy?: One of five pitchers (including closer Rick Aguilera) traded by the Mets to the Twins for Frank Viola in 1989; has recorded more wins than Viola in each of the last three years

Steve **Bridge Too** Farr

What: Relief pitcher

When: 1984-present

Where: Cleveland, Kansas City, New York Yankees

Why Should I Know This Guy?: Four seasons, twenty or more saves; performs better in even-numbered years

Brian **Deer** Hunter

What: First base

When: 1991-present

Where: Atlanta, Pittsburgh

Why Should I Know This Guy?: Hit a home run in the 1991 World Series

Jose **Blame It on** Rijo

What: Starting pitcher

When: 1984-present

Where: New York Yankees, Oakland, Cincinnati

Why Should I Know This Guy?: In six years with Reds, has never had an ERA over 3.00

"Down to our last out, but we're...
stayin' alive...
stayin' alive..."

JIM "SATURDAY NIGHT" LEFEBVRE

Jim **Saturday Night** Lefebvre

What: Infield; manager
When: 1965-72;1989-93
Where: Los Angeles; Seattle, Chicago Cubs
Why Should I Know This Guy?: Was second baseman in an all-switch-hitting infield with the Dodgers

Ruben **High** Sierra

What: Outfield, DH
When: 1986-present
Where: Texas, Oakland
Why Should I Know This Guy?: Has driven in over 100 runs in every other year of his career, including 101 in 1993

Jerry **Rats** Willard

What: Catcher
When: 1984-present
Where: Cleveland, Oakland, Chicago White Sox, Atlanta, Montreal, Seattle
Why Should I Know This Guy?: Of 24 career home runs, 10 came as a rookie

CRAIG "**MATINEE AT THE**" BIGGIO

Craig **Matinee at the** Biggio
What: Second base, used to be a catcher
When: 1988-present
Where: Houston
Why Should I Know This Guy?: Played in every game for the Astros, 1992

TV Reruns

Mike **Car 54** LaValliere
What: Catcher
When: 1984-present
Where: Philadelphia, St. Louis, Pittsburgh, Chicago White Sox
Why Should I Know This Guy?: Affectionately known as Spanky; son of minor-league catcher Guy LaValliere

Brady **Bunch** Anderson

What: Outfield

When: 1988-present

Where: Boston, Baltimore

Why Should I Know This Guy?:

Drove in 80 runs as a leadoff hitter, 1992

Greg **Life of** Briley

What: Outfield

When: 1988-present

Where: Seattle, Florida

Why Should I Know This Guy?:

Moved from baseball's northernmost team to its southernmost in 1993

Joe Slusarski **and Hutch**

What: Starting pitcher

When: 1991-present

Where: Oakland

Why Should I Know This Guy?:

Member of the 1988 U.S. Olympic baseball team

Harold **Growing** Baines

What: DH, outfield

When: 1980-present

Where: Chicago White Sox, Texas, Oakland, Baltimore

Why Should I Know This Guy?:

White Sox career home run leader, without ever hitting over 30 in a season

Cecil Espy **N**

What: Outfield

When: 1983-present

Where: Los Angeles, Texas, Pittsburgh

Why Should I Know This Guy?:

Caught stealing 20 times with the Rangers in 1989, to lead the league

Alan **Have Gun, Will** Trammell

What: Shortstop

When: 1977-present

Where: Detroit

Why Should I Know This Guy?:

He and Lou Whitaker make up the longest-standing double play combination in major-league history

Mike Hartley, **Mike Hartley**

What: Relief pitcher

When: 1989-present

Where: Los Angeles, Philadelphia, Minnesota

Why Should I Know This Guy?:

Threw a complete-game shutout for the Dodgers, 1990

Joe **Leave It to** Boever

What: Relief pitcher
When: 1985-present
Where: St. Louis, Atlanta, Philadelphia, Houston, Oakland, Detroit
Why Should I Know This Guy?: Pitched in half of the Astros' games in 1992, to lead the league in appearances

B.J. **and the Bear** Surhoff

What: Third base, outfield, used to catch
When: 1987-present
Where: Milwaukee
Why Should I Know This Guy?: Had career highs in at bats, hits, runs, doubles, home runs, and RBIs in 1993; father played basketball in the NBA

Classic Characters

Darryl **Gomer** Kile

What: Pitcher

When: 1991-present

Where: Houston

Why Should I Know This Guy?:

Led league with 15 hit batters in 1993

Joe **Sergeant** Carter

What: Outfield

When: 1983-present

Where: Chicago Cubs, Cleveland, San Diego, Toronto

Why Should I Know This Guy?:

Not just a one (Series-winning) homer wonder, he's averaged more than 100 RBIs a year over the last nine seasons

ChrisNamesChrisNamesChrisNamesChrisNames

FLO

"You're confined to the base!"

JOE "SERGEANT" CARTER

ChrisNamesChrisNamesChrisNamesChrisNames

DARRYL "GOMER" KILE

ChrisNamesChrisNamesChrisNamesChrisNamesChrisNamesChrisNamesChrisNames

For Brett, tomorrow is another (good) day (to play two).

BRETT **"TARA"** BUTLER

ChrisNamesChrisNamesChrisNamesChrisNamesChrisNamesChrisNamesChrisNames

ChrisNamesChrisNamesChrisNamesChrisNames

Brett **Tara** Butler

What: Outfield

When: 1981-present

Where: Atlanta, Cleveland, San Francisco, Los Angeles

Why Should I Know This Guy?: Refused Ted Turner's request that he change his name to Rhett

Scott Fletcher **Christian**

What: Second base

When: 1981-present

Where: Chicago Cubs, Texas, Chicago White Sox, Milwaukee, Boston

Why Should I Know This Guy?: Thirty-three of his 90 career stolen bases have come in the last two years

Joe **Colonel** Klink

What: Relief pitcher

When: 1987-present

Where: Minnesota, Oakland, Florida

Why Should I Know This Guy?: Has 10 career wins, all with the A's in 1991

ChrisNamesChrisNamesChrisNamesChrisNames

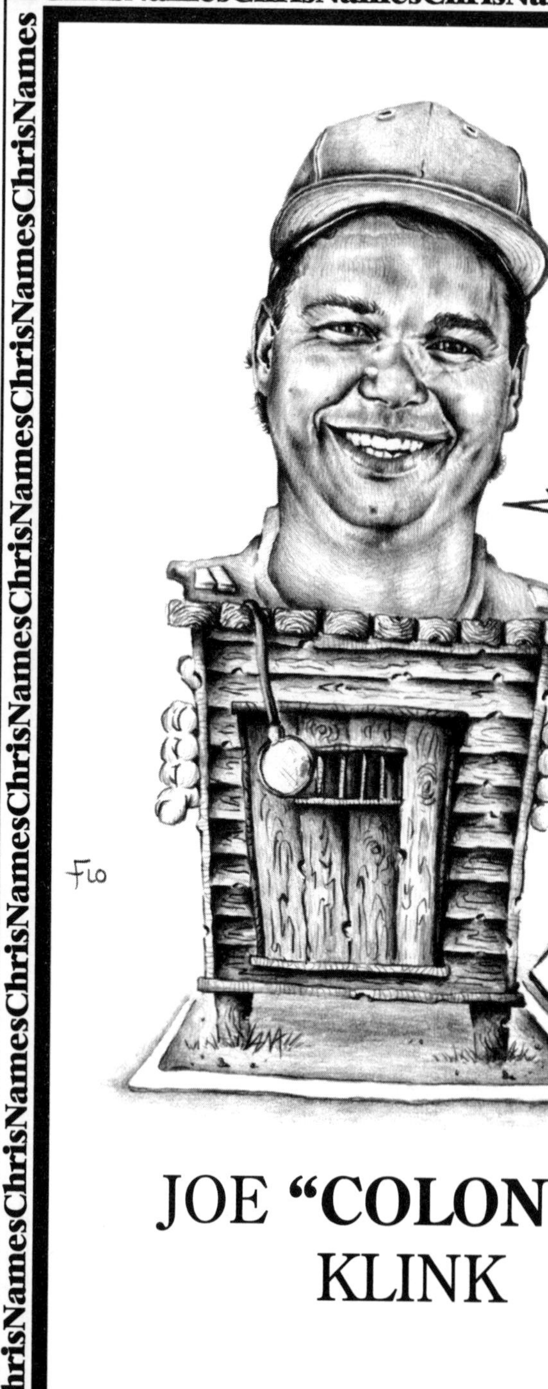

JOE "COLONEL" KLINK

Brook Jacoby **Wan Kenobi**

What: Third base

When: 1981-92

Where: Atlanta, Cleveland, Oakland

Why Should I Know This Guy?:

Two-time All-Star; signed with Chunichi Dragons of Japan after 1992 season

Mark **Officer** Lemke

What: Second base

When: 1988-present

Where: Atlanta

Why Should I Know This Guy?:

Batted .417 in the 1991 World Series

Chris **Mr.** Haney

What: Starting pitcher

When: 1991-present

Where: Montreal, Kansas City

Why Should I Know This Guy?:

Threw shutouts for the Royals in 1992 and 1993

ChrisNamesChrisNamesChrisNamesChrisNamesChrisNamesChrisNamesChrisNamesChrisNames

ChrisNamesChrisNamesChrisNamesChrisNamesChrisNamesChrisNamesChrisNamesChrisNames

This guy knows how to spend his off days.

JAY **"FERRIS"** BUHNER

Jay **Ferris** Buhner

What: Outfield

When: 1987-present

Where: New York Yankees, Seattle

Why Should I Know This Guy?:

Had career highs of 27 home runs, 98 RBIs, and 91 runs scored in 1993

Scott Livingstone, **I Presume**

What: Third base

When: 1991-present

Where: Detroit, San Diego

Why Should I Know This Guy?:

Career .288 batting average

Mark **Chauncy** Gardner

What: Starting pitcher

When: 1989-present

Where: Montreal, Kansas City, Florida

Why Should I Know This Guy?:

Of seven wins in 1990, three were complete-game shutouts

Actors and Directors

Jim **Hey** Abbott

What: Starting pitcher

When: 1989-present

Where: California, New York Yankees

Why Should I Know This Guy?:

No-hitter, 1993

Dave **Ingmar** Bergman

What: First base, outfield

When: 1977-92

Where: New York Yankees, Houston, San Francisco, Detroit

Why Should I Know This Guy?:

College All-American at Illinois State University, 1974

Andy **Dick** Van Slyke

What: Outfield

When: 1983-present

Where: St. Louis, Pittsburgh

Why Should I Know This Guy?:

Gold Glove winner, 1988-92

Scott **Tallulah** Bankhead

What: Pitcher

When: 1986-present

Where: Kansas City, Seattle, Cincinnati, Boston

Why Should I Know This Guy?: Member of 1984 U.S. Olympic baseball team

Tim **Eli** Wallach

What: Third base

When: 1980-present

Where: Montreal, Los Angeles

Why Should I Know This Guy?: Has averaged 565 at bats per season over the last twelve years

Jim **Bella** Fregosi

What: Infield; manager

When: 1961-78; 1978-81, 1986-88, 1991-present

Where: California, New York Mets, Texas, Pittsburgh; California, Chicago White Sox, Philadelphia

Why Should I Know This Guy?: Hired three times as a midseason managerial replacement

4.
Emphatic Names

Glenn **No** Braggs **Just Fact**

What: Outfield

When: 1986-92

Where: Milwaukee, Cincinnati

Why Should I Know This Guy?:

Signed with Taiyo Whales of Japan after 1992 season

ChrisNamesChrisNamesChrisNamesChrisNames

GREG GAGNE
"WITH A SPOON"

Greg Gagne **with a Spoon**

What: Shortstop
When: 1983-present
Where: Minnesota, Kansas City
Why Should I Know This Guy?:
Royals Player of the Year in 1993

Tim Leary **Is Not Dead**

What: Pitcher
When: 1981-present
Where: New York Mets, Milwaukee, Los Angeles, Cincinnati, New York Yankees, Seattle, Montreal
Why Should I Know This Guy?:
Led National League with 15 intentional walks in 1990

Matt **No** Nokes

What: Catcher, DH
When: 1985-present
Where: San Francisco, Detroit, New York Yankees
Why Should I Know This Guy?:
Had a great year for the Tigers in 1987 – 32 home runs, 87 RBIs, .289 average

KEVIN "TOTALLY" GROSS

Kevin **Totally** Gross

What: Starting pitcher
When: 1983-present
Where: Philadelphia, Montreal, Los Angeles
Why Should I Know This Guy?: Has led the league in hit batters three times – 1986, 1987, 1988

Kevin **No** Maas

What: DH, first base
When: 1990-present
Where: New York Yankees, San Diego
Why Should I Know This Guy?: Hit 21 homers in 254 at bats as a rookie

Mike **Horse** Fetters

What: Relief pitcher
When: 1989-present
Where: California, Milwaukee
Why Should I Know This Guy?: Posted a 1.87 ERA in 50 appearances with the Brewers in 1992

Gary **Great** Scott

What: Third base

When: 1991-present

Where: Chicago Cubs, San Francisco

Why Should I Know This Guy?:

In the Marlins organization in 1993; trying to make it with the Giants in 1994

5.
Historical

American History

Bill **One If By** Landrum

What: Relief pitcher
When: 1987-present
Where: Cincinnati, Chicago Cubs, Pittsburgh, Montreal
Why Should I Know This Guy?: Accumulated 56 saves in three years with the Pirates, 1989-91

Jimmy **Francis Scott** Key

What: Starting pitcher

When: 1984-present

Where: Toronto, New York Yankees

Why Should I Know This Guy?:

Has a career winning percentage of .606 – better than Walter Johnson or Steve Carlton

Roberto **Remember the** Alomar

What: Second base

When: 1988-present

Where: San Diego, Toronto

Why Should I Know This Guy?:

Son of major-leaguer Sandy Alomar; proves that Darwin's theory of evolution applies to second basemen

ChrisNamesChrisNamesChrisNamesChrisNames

ChrisNamesChrisNamesChrisNamesChrisNamesChrisNamesChrisNamesChrisNames

They're back, back, back, back, back...
at the warning track, at the wall...

SANDY "REMEMBER THE OTHER" ALOMAR, JR.

ChrisNamesChrisNamesChrisNamesChrisNamesChrisNamesChrisNamesChrisNames

ChrisNamesChrisNamesChrisNamesChrisNames

Sandy **Remember the Other**
Alomar, Jr.

What: Catcher

When: 1988-present

Where: San Diego, Cleveland

Why Should I Know This Guy?:
Single-handedly responsible for a national rise in health-insurance premiums, due to persistent injuries as Tribe backstop

Paul Molitor **and the Merrimac**

What: DH, first base, and about everywhere else at some point

When: 1978-present

Where: Milwaukee, Toronto

Why Should I Know This Guy?:
World Series MVP in his first season with Toronto, after fifteen years as a star for the Brewers

He's setting up a target in the strike zone...

BRENT "REMEMBER THE" MAYNE

Greg **Appa** Maddux

What: Starting pitcher

When: 1986-present

Where: Chicago Cubs, Atlanta

Why Should I Know This Guy?:

Not only good, but durable – has led the National League in innings pitched for three consecutive seasons

Sam **Little Big** Horn

What: DH, outfield

When: 1987-present

Where: Boston, Baltimore, Cleveland, New York Yankees

Why Should I Know This Guy?:

Hit 23 home runs in 317 at bats for the Orioles in 1991

Brent **Remember the** Mayne

What: Catcher

When: 1990-present

Where: Kansas City

Why Should I Know This Guy?:

Drew more intentional walks per plate appearance than Albert Belle in 1993

John **I Am Not a** Kruk

What: First base

When: 1986-present

Where: San Diego, Philadelphia

Why Should I Know This Guy?:

Stole 18 bases for the Padres in 1987

International

Tony **Prehistoric** Fossas

What: Relief pitcher

When: 1988-present

Where: Texas, Milwaukee, Boston

Why Should I Know This Guy?:

Broke into the majors as a 30-year-old rookie

Todd **Aris** Stottlemyre

What: Starting pitcher

When: 1988-present

Where: Toronto

Why Should I Know This Guy?:

Gave up his 1,000th hit in 1993

ChrisNamesChrisNamesChrisNamesChrisNames

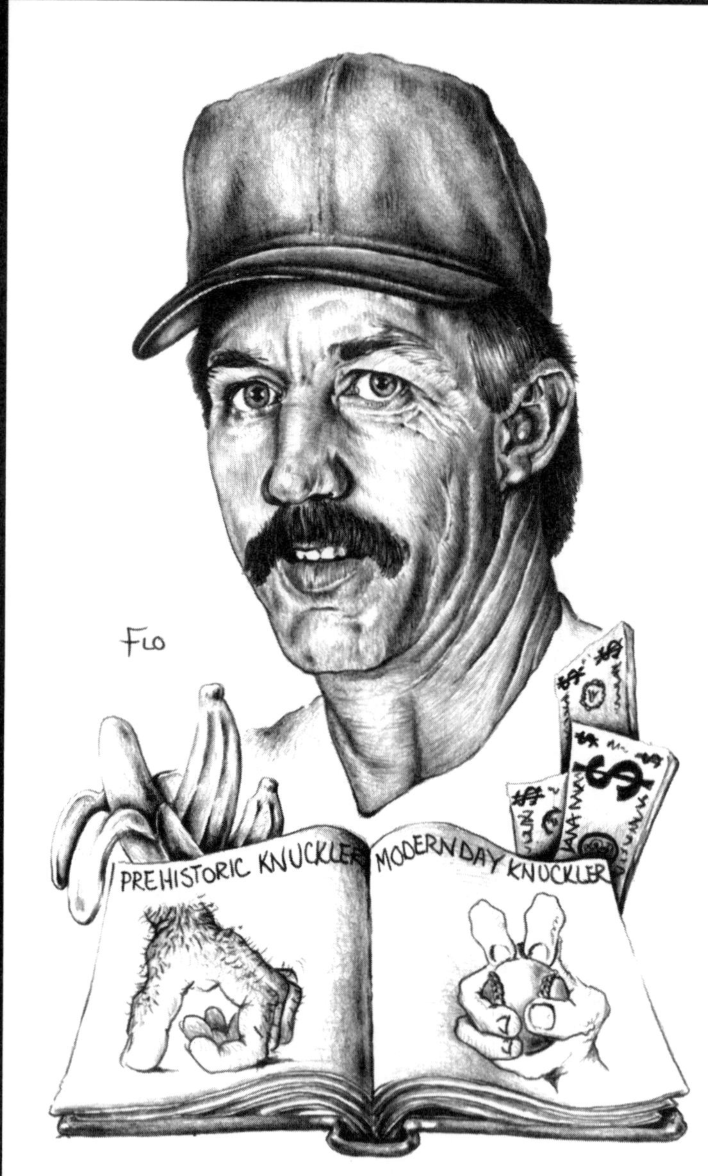

DANNY DARWIN
"THEORY"

Danny Darwin **Theory**

What: Pitcher
When: 1978-present
Where: Texas, Milwaukee, Houston, Boston
Why Should I Know This Guy?:
Had a career-high 15 wins in 1993, at the age of 37

Denny **Wailing** Walling

What: Third base, first base, outfield
When: 1975-92
Where: Oakland, Houston, St. Louis, Texas
Why Should I Know This Guy?:
Hit .312 with 13 home runs and 58 RBIs for the Astros in 1986 – all career highs

Bobby **Tokyo** Rose

What: Infield
When: 1989-92
Where: California
Why Should I Know This Guy?:
Sold by Angels to Taiyo Whales of Japan after 1992 season

ChrisNamesChrisNamesChrisNamesChrisNames

ChrisNamesChrisNamesChrisNamesChrisNamesChrisNamesChrisNamesChrisNamesChrisNamesChrisNamesChrisNamesChrisNames

ChrisNamesChrisNamesChrisNamesChrisNamesChrisNamesChrisNamesChrisNamesChrisNamesChrisNamesChrisNamesChrisNames

Chevy Chase was wrong. ..... Franco's not dead, he just signed with the White Sox as a free agent.

JULIO
"GENERALISSIMO"
FRANCO

ChrisNamesChrisNamesChrisNamesChrisNames

Benito **Il Duce** Santiago

What: Catcher

When: 1986-present

Where: San Diego, Florida

Why Should I Know This Guy?:

Career batting record suspiciously similar to Tony Pena's

Julio **Generalissimo** Franco

What: DH

When: 1982-present

Where: Philadelphia, Cleveland, Texas, Chicago White Sox

Why Should I Know This Guy?:

Career batting average at the end of 1993 season was .2999

Phil **Final** Plantier

What: Outfield

When: 1990-present

Where: Boston, San Diego

Why Should I Know This Guy?:

Hit 34 home runs for the Padres in 1993 – 16 more than he'd had in two previous seasons with the Red Sox

ChrisNamesChrisNamesChrisNamesChrisNames

BENITO "IL DUCE" SANTIAGO

6.
Food and Drink

Breakfast

Sid **Coffee and** Bream

What: First baseman
When: 1983-present
Where: Los Angeles, Pittsburgh, Atlanta, Houston
Why should I know this guy?:
Set National League record for assists in a season by a first baseman – 166 for Pirates in 1986

Johnny **Quaker** Oates

What: Catcher; manager

When: 1970-81; 1991-present

Where: Baltimore, Atlanta, Philadelphia, Los Angeles, New York Yankees; Baltimore

Why should I know this guy?: Was only manager in the majors not to call for at least one squeeze play in 1993

Mike **Leggo** Gallego

What: Utility infielder

When: 1989-present

Where: Oakland, New York Yankees

Why should I know this guy?: His .287 batting average in 1993 was a career high

Snacks

Jim **Frito** Leyritz

What: First base, catcher, outfield, DH

When: 1990-present

Where: New York Yankees

Why should I know this guy?:

Had a career year in 1993, with a .309 average and 14 home runs in 259 at bats

Chito **Goes Crunch** Martinez

What: Outfield

When: 1991-present

Where: Baltimore, New York Yankees

Why should I know this guy?:

In 1993 there were more Martinezes in the majors than Joneses

Paul **Orville** Assenmacher

What: Relief pitcher

When: 1986-present

Where: Atlanta, Chicago Cubs, New York Yankees, Chicago White Sox

Why should I know this guy?:

In eight years and 531 appearances in the majors, has had one start

Jim Lindeman **Cheese**

What: First base

When: 1986-present

Where: St. Louis, Detroit, Philadelphia, Houston, New York Mets

Why Should I Know This Guy?:

Has totaled 539 at bats in eight major-league seasons

Kevin Ritz **Cracker**

What: Pitcher

When: 1989-92

Where: Detroit

Why Should I Know This Guy?:

In the Rockies organization in 1993

Fruits and Vegetables

Glenallen **Strawberry** Hill

What: Outfield

When: 1989-present

Where: Toronto, Cleveland, Chicago Cubs

Why Should I Know This Guy?:

Trying to overcome the jinx on highly touted outfielders from the Blue Jays organization

Henry **Ava** Cotto

What: Outfield

When: 1984-present

Where: Chicago Cubs, New York Yankees, Seattle, Florida, Baltimore

Why Should I Know This Guy?:

Has a better career stolen-base percentage than Rickey Henderson

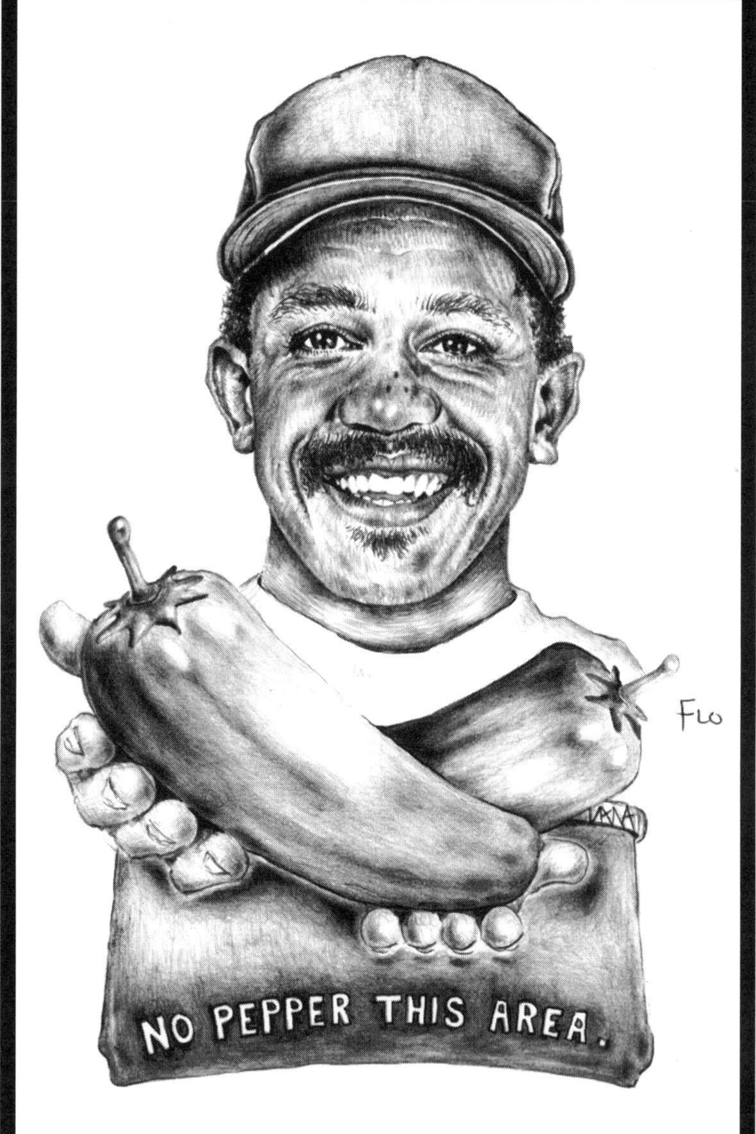

TONY **"JALA"** PENA

Tony **Jala** Pena

What: Catcher

When: 1980-present

Where: Pittsburgh, St. Louis, Boston, Cleveland

Why Should I Know This Guy?:

The Cardinals traded Andy Van Slyke and Mike LaValliere to get him from the Pirates on April Fool's Day, 1987

Wade **Cranberry** Boggs

What: Third base

When: 1982-present

Where: Boston, New York Yankees

Why Should I Know This Guy?:

Led the majors for six consecutive years in intentional walks, 1987-92

Meat Dishes

Bill **Veal** Pecota

What: Infield

When: 1986-present

Where: Kansas City, New York Mets, Atlanta

Why Should I Know This Guy?:
Hit .323 as Terry Pendleton's backup in 1993

Hector **Sizzling** Fajardo

What: Pitcher

When: 1991-present

Where: Pittsburgh, Texas

Why Should I Know This Guy?:
Has pitched with eight different minor-league teams, as well as the Pirates and Rangers, in the past three years

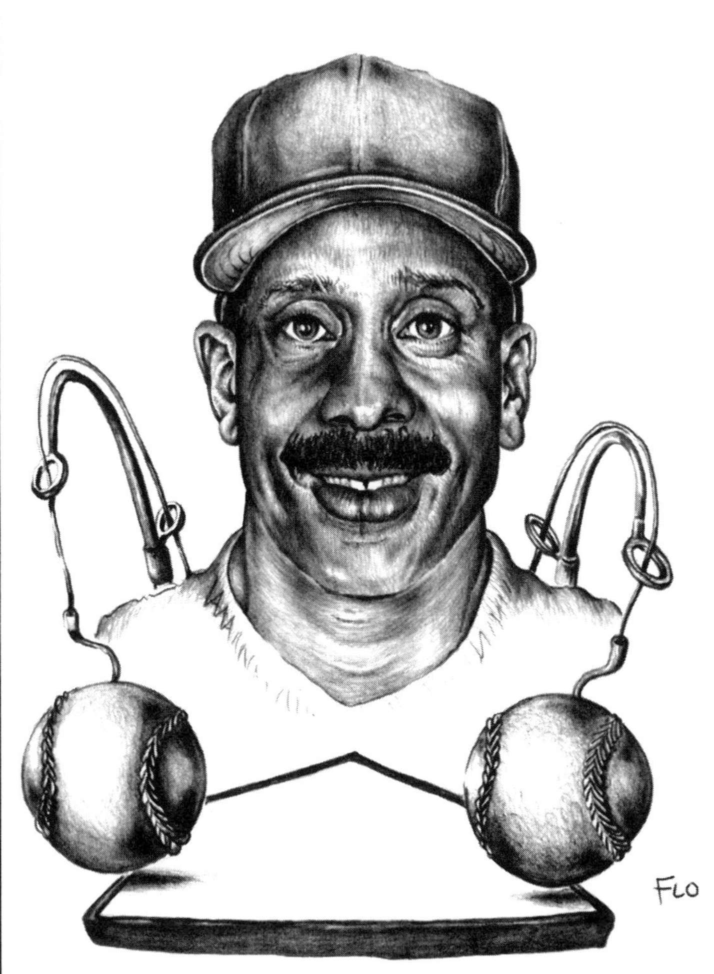

Nibble the corners a little with him...

KEVIN “SMALLMOUTH” BASS

Kevin **Smallmouth** Bass

What: Outfield

When: 1982-present

Where: Milwaukee, Houston, San Francisco, New York Mets

Why Should I Know This Guy?: Had career year with the Astros in 1986: .311 average, 20 home runs, 22 stolen bases

Chris Hammond **Cheese**

What: Starting pitcher

When: 1990-present

Where: Cincinnati, Florida

Why Should I Know This Guy?: Led Marlins in wins in 1993

Joey **Alba** Cora

What: Second base

When: 1987-present

Where: San Diego, Chicago White Sox

Why Should I Know This Guy?: Led the American League in sacrifices, 1993

Jose Lind **Cuisine**

What: Second base
When: 1987-present
Where: Pittsburgh, Kansas City
Why Should I Know This Guy?:
Proof that even if Roberto Alomar couldn't hit, he'd still be making millions of dollars

Paul **Veal** Sorrento

What: First base
When: 1989-present
Where: Minnesota, Cleveland
Why Should I Know This Guy?:
Hit 16 of his 18 home runs in 1993 versus right-handed pitching

ChrisNamesChrisNamesChrisNamesChrisNamesChrisNamesChrisNamesChrisNames

ChrisNamesChrisNamesChrisNamesChrisNamesChrisNamesChrisNamesChrisNames

He lives on a steady diet of groundballs.

JOSE LIND "CUISINE"

ChrisNamesChrisNamesChrisNamesChrisNames

Side Orders

Fettucine Alfredo Griffin

What: Shortstop, second base

When: 1976-93

Where: Cleveland, Toronto, Oakland, Los Angeles

Why Should I Know This Guy?:
Was Rookie of the Year with Blue Jays in 1979; rejoined them to play on World Series winners of 1992 and 1993

Red Hot Chili Davis

What: DH, outfield

When: 1981-present

Where: San Francisco, California, Minnesota

Why Should I Know This Guy?:
Led the Angels with 112 RBIs in 1993

Royce **A Roni** Clayton **the San Francisco Treat**

What: Shortstop

When: 1991-present

Where: San Francisco

Why Should I Know This Guy?:

Turned 103 double plays in 1993, to tie Jay Bell for most in the National League

Dave **Prince** Righetti

What: Pitcher

When: 1979-present

Where: New York Yankees, San Francisco, Oakland

Why Should I Know This Guy?:

Going into 1994 season, had these career stats: 3.33 ERA, 252 saves, 1333.1 innings pitched, 5,665 batters faced, 555 runs allowed, 494 earned runs allowed – all palindromic numbers

Suds

Steve **Head for the Mountains of** Buechele

What: Third base

When: 1985-present

Where: Texas, Pittsburgh, Chicago Cubs

Why Should I Know This Guy?: Average of .272 in 1993 was a career high

Jeff **When You're Having More Than One** Schaefer

What: Infield

When: 1989-92

Where: Chicago White Sox, Seattle

Why Should I Know This Guy?: Spent nine years in minors before White Sox called him up as a 29-year-old rookie in 1989

Jeff Torborg **Gold**

What: Catcher; manager

When: 1964-73; 1977-79, 1989-93

Where: Los Angeles, California; Cleveland, Chicago White Sox, New York Mets

Why Should I Know This Guy?: Named American League Manager of the Year with White Sox in 1990

Gregg Olson **Golden**

What: Closer

When: 1988-present

Where: Baltimore, Atlanta

Why Should I Know This Guy?: In five years as Orioles' closer, averaged 32 saves and a 2.23 ERA

The Hard Stuff

Kal **Jack** Daniels

What: Outfield

When: 1986-92

Where: Cincinnati, Los Angeles, Chicago Cubs

Why Should I Know This Guy?: Full first name is Kalvoski

Dave **Vodka** Martinez

What: Outfield

When: 1986-present

Where: Chicago Cubs, Montreal, Cincinnati, San Francisco

Why Should I Know This Guy?: Likes to be shaken, not stirred

ChrisNamesChrisNamesChrisNamesChrisNames

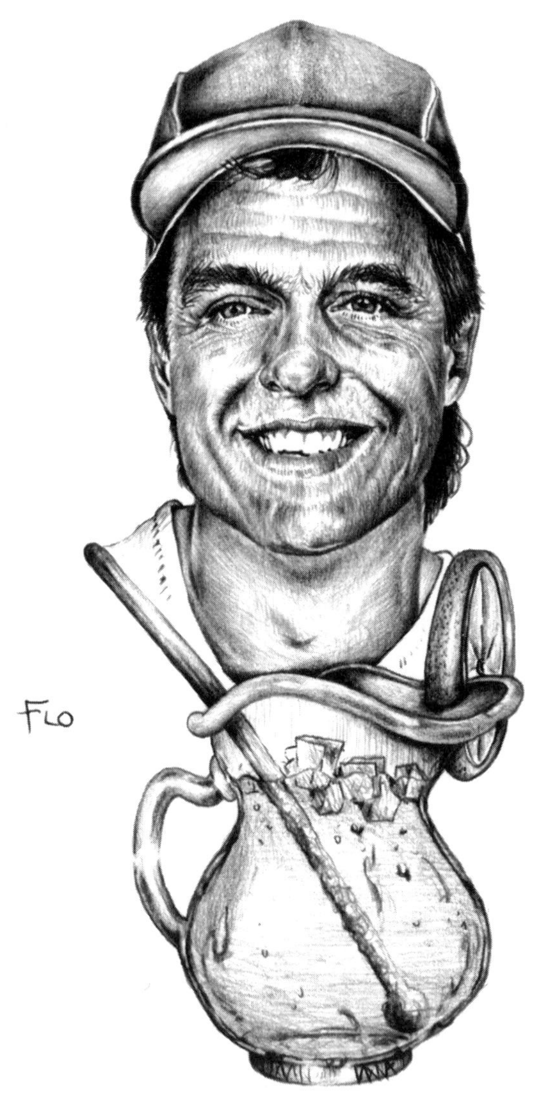

Get a relief pitcher in there for him...

FRANK TANANA
"DAIQUIRI"

ChrisNamesChrisNamesChrisNamesChrisNamesChrisNamesChrisNamesChrisNamesChrisNames

ChrisNamesChrisNamesChrisNamesChrisNamesChrisNamesChrisNamesChrisNamesChrisNames

ChrisNamesChrisNamesChrisNamesChrisNames

Frank Tanana **Daiquiri**

What: Starting pitcher

When: 1973-93

Where: California, Boston, Texas, Detroit, New York Mets, New York Yankees

Why Should I Know This Guy?:
In 21 seasons accumulated 240 wins and 2,773 strikeouts, while transforming from power pitcher to finesse pitcher

Chris **Bartles and** James

What: Outfield

When: 1986-present

Where: Philadelphia, San Diego, Cleveland, San Francisco, Houston, Texas

Why Should I Know This Guy?:
Had best season with the Indians in 1990: .299 average and 70 RBIs

GEORGE "TACO" BELL

Fast Food

Eric **Burger** King

What: Pitcher

When: 1986-92

Where: Detroit, Chicago White Sox, Cleveland

Why Should I Know This Guy?: Was 11-4 as a rookie with the Tigers

George **Taco** Bell

What: DH, outfield

When: 1981-present

Where: Toronto, Chicago Cubs, Chicago White Sox

Why Should I Know This Guy?: American League MVP in 1987; has grounded into more double plays than he's hit home runs for the past two seasons

You putting anything on that ball?...

TOM "COTTON" CANDIOTTI

Reggie **Colonel** Sanders
What: Outfield
When: 1991-present
Where: Cincinnati
Why Should I Know This Guy?:
Had 20 home runs, 27 stolen bases in 1993

Sweets

Tom **Cotton** Candiotti
What: Starting pitcher
When: 1983-present
Where: Milwaukee, Cleveland, Toronto, Los Angeles
Why Should I Know This Guy?:
Pitched 17 complete games for the Indians in 1986

Peter **Chips A** Hoy
What: Relief pitcher
When: 1992
Where: Boston
Why Should I Know This Guy?:
Member of the 1988 Canadian Olympic baseball team

Scott **Am** Brosius

What: Outfield, third base

When: 1991-present

Where: Oakland

Why Should I Know This Guy?:

Has only been caught stealing once in 13 career attempts going into 1994 season

Eating Out

Dennis **Short Order** Cook

What: Pitcher

When: 1988-present

Where: San Francisco, Philadelphia, Los Angeles, Cleveland, Chicago White Sox

Why Should I Know This Guy?:

Led the Amercian League with five balks in 1992

ChrisNamesChrisNamesChrisNamesChrisNames

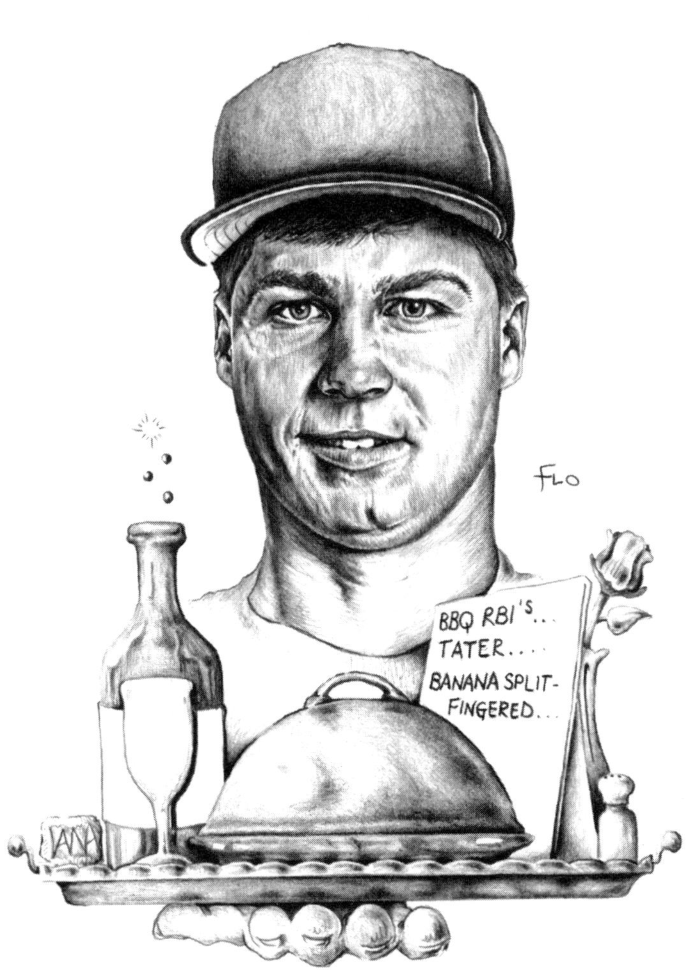

SCOTT "ROOM" SERVAIS

ChrisNamesChrisNamesChrisNamesChrisNames

Scott **Room** Servais

What: Catcher
When: 1991-present
Where: Houston
Why Should I Know This Guy?:
Hasn't attempted a stolen base in 178 games in the majors

Pat **Pick Up the** Tabler

What: Infield, outfield
When: 1981-92
Where: Chicago Cubs, Cleveland, Kansas City, New York Mets, Toronto
Why Should I Know This Guy?:
Has a career .500 batting average with the bases loaded

7.
Musical

Bands

Rob **AC** Ducey

What: Outfield

When: 1987-present

Where: Toronto, California, Texas

Why Should I Know This Guy?:

Has yet to have a season with 100 major-league at bats

Craig **Brewer and** Shipley

What: Infield

When: 1986-present

Where: Los Angeles, New York Mets, San Diego

Why Should I Know This Guy?:

Native of Sydney, Australia; 105 at bats in 1993 were his most ever in the majors

Rafael **Emerson, Lake and** Palmeiro

What: First base

When: 1986-present

Where: Chicago Cubs, Texas, Baltimore

Why Should I Know This Guy?:

He and Will Clark starred together in college at Mississippi State

Jamie **Men at** Quirk

What: Catcher, infield, outfield

When: 1975-92

Where: Kansas City, Milwaukee, St. Louis, Chicago White Sox, Cleveland, Oakland, Baltimore

Why Should I Know This Guy?: In the early '70s, was sometimes mistaken for George Brett

Dion James **and the Belmonts**

What: Outfield

When: 1983-93

Where: Milwaukee, Atlanta, Cleveland, New York Yankees

Why Should I Know This Guy?: Hit .332 for the Yankees in 1993; will try to do the same for the Chunichi Dragons of Japan in 1994

ChrisNamesChrisNamesChrisNamesChrisNamesChrisNamesChrisNamesChrisNamesChrisNames

This group must be the result of some stolen "basses."

CHUCK
"NEW KIDS ON THE"
KNOBLAUCH

ChrisNamesChrisNamesChrisNamesChrisNamesChrisNamesChrisNamesChrisNamesChrisNames

Chuck **New Kids on the** Knoblauch

What: Second base

When: 1991-present

Where: Minnesota

Why Should I Know This Guy?:

American League Rookie of the Year, 1991

Shane **Fleetwood** Mack

What: Outfield

When: 1987-present

Where: San Diego, Minnesota

Why Should I Know This Guy?:

Hit by pitches 15 times in 1992 to lead American League

Ted **Tower of** Power

What: Relief pitcher

When: 1981-present

Where: Los Angeles, Cincinnati, Kansas City, Detroit, St. Louis, Pittsburgh, Cleveland, Seattle

Why Should I Know This Guy?:

Had 13 saves in last two months of the 1993 season for the Mariners

ChrisNamesChrisNamesChrisNamesChrisNames

TED "TOWER OF" POWER

Kirby Puckett **and the Union Gap**

What: Outfield

When: 1984-present

Where: Minnesota

Why Should I Know This Guy?:

Four hits away from 2,000 going into the 1994 season; Bob Costas gave a son the middle name Kirby in his honor

Bob Melvin **and the Blue Notes**

What: Catcher

When: 1985-present

Where: Detroit, San Francisco, Baltimore, Kansas City, Boston

Why Should I Know This Guy?:

Has only been hit by a pitch once in nine seasons

Eric **Little** Anthony **and the Imperials**

What: Outfield

When: 1989-present

Where: Houston, Seattle

Why Should I Know This Guy?:

Going from a tough dome to an easy one in 1994

Craig **Def** Lefferts

What: Pitcher
When: 1983-present
Where: Chicago Cubs, San Diego, San Francisco, Baltimore, Texas, California
Why Should I Know This Guy?: In 11 years has pitched 1,111 innings

Jeff Juden **Priest**

What: Pitcher
When: 1991-present
Where: Houston, Philadelphia
Why Should I Know This Guy?: One of the biggest pitchers (6′7″, 245 lbs.) to toe the rubber

Mike **Loggins and** Mussina

What: Starting pitcher
When: 1991-present
Where: Baltimore
Why Should I Know This Guy?: Had 18 wins in 1992

Bill Doran **Duran**

What: Second base

When: 1982-present

Where: Houston, Cincinnati, Milwaukee

Why Should I Know This Guy?: Led National League second basemen with a .992 fielding percentage in 1987

Tim **Golden** Naehring

What: Second base

When: 1990-present

Where: Boston

Why Should I Know This Guy?: One-for-one in career stolen-base attempts

Solo Acts

Patrick **Imagine** Lennon

What: Outfield, first base

When: 1991-92

Where: Seattle

Why Should I Know This Guy?: His one career hit is a double

Charlie **Isaac** Hayes

What: Third base

When: 1988-present

Where: San Francisco, Philadelphia, New York Yankees, Colorado

Why Should I Know This Guy?:
Led National League with 45 doubles in 1993

Donovan Osborne **The Hurdy Gurdy Man**

What: Starting pitcher

When: 1992-present

Where: St. Louis

Why Should I Know This Guy?:
Has a 21-16 record over two seasons

Barry **U.S.** Bonds

What: Outfield

When: 1986-present

Where: Pittsburgh, San Francisco

Why Should I Know This Guy?:

His 46 home runs, 123 RBIs, and .336 average in 1993 were all better than the numbers Carl Yastrzemski posted to win baseball's last triple crown in 1967

Mark **Woody** Guthrie

What: Pitcher

When: 1989-present

Where: Minnesota

Why Should I Know This Guy?:

Innings pitched have declined for four straight years

Bob **Ebony Eyes** Welch

What: Starting pitcher

When: 1978-present

Where: Los Angeles, Oakland

Why Should I Know This Guy?:

Twenty-seven wins for the A's in 1990 is the most in the league since Denny McLain had 31 in 1968

Mike **The Thriller** Jackson

What: Relief pitcher

When: 1986-present

Where: Philadelphia, Seattle, San Francisco

Why Should I Know This Guy?:

Led the majors in appearances, 1993

Luis **Ap-** Polonia

What: Outfield

When: 1987-present

Where: Oakland, New York Yankees, California

Why Should I Know This Guy?:

Has led the American League in times caught stealing for three straight seasons

Stan Belinda **Carlisle**

What: Relief pitcher
When: 1989-present
Where: Pittsburgh, Kansas City
Why Should I Know This Guy?:
Used to be a boxer

Wally **Lionel** Ritchie

What: Relief pitcher
When: 1987-92
Where: Philadelphia,
Chicago White Sox
Why Should I Know This Guy?:
Threw a no-hitter for Scranton of the International League in 1990

Lee **Cat** Stevens

What: First base
When: 1990-92
Where: California
Why Should I Know This Guy?:
Apparently a prime reason why the Angels traded for J.T. Snow

ChrisNamesChrisNamesChrisNamesChrisNamesChrisNamesChrisNamesChrisNamesChrisNamesChrisNamesChrisNamesChrisNames

Grab some "wood stock" and "lay us" down a perfect bunt.

SCOTT **"LAY LADY"**
LEIUS

ChrisNamesChrisNamesChrisNamesChrisNamesChrisNamesChrisNamesChrisNamesChrisNamesChrisNamesChrisNamesChrisNames

ChrisNamesChrisNamesChrisNamesChrisNames

Kenny **The Gambler** Rogers

What: Pitcher

When: 1989-present

Where: Texas

Why Should I Know This Guy?:

Led the American League with five balks in 1993

Major Lance Johnson

What: Outfield

When: 1987-present

Where: St. Louis, Chicago White Sox

Why Should I Know This Guy?:

Has led the American League in triples for each of the last three years

Sounds of the '60s

Scott **Lay Lady** Leius

What: Shortstop, third base

When: 1990-present

Where: Minnesota

Why Should I Know This Guy?:

Supposed to be Twins shortstop, but was injured most of 1993

Charles Nagy**'s Farm**

What: Starting pitcher

When: 1990-present

Where: Cleveland

Why Should I Know This Guy?:

Supposed to be Indians ace, but was injured most of 1993

Riders on the Storm Davis

What: Pitcher

When: 1982-present

Where: Baltimore, San Diego, Oakland, Kansas City, Detroit

Why Should I Know This Guy?:

Won 19 games in 1989; won just 19 more in the four subsequent seasons

Donn **Whiter Shade of** Pall

What: Relief pitcher

When: 1988-present

Where: Chicago White Sox, Philadelphia, New York Yankees

Why Should I Know This Guy?:

Posted the best ERA on the Phillies in 1993

Von **Purple** Hayes

What: Outfield, first base

When: 1981-92

Where: Cleveland, Philadelphia, California

Why Should I Know This Guy?:

Traded by the Indians to the Phillies for five players – including future batting champion Julio Franco – in 1982

Bud **Paint It** Black

What: Starting pitcher

When: 1981-present

Where: Seattle, Kansas City, Cleveland, Toronto, San Francisco

Why Should I Know This Guy?:

In 1993, he picked off more runners (5) than were thrown out by his catcher trying to steal (3).

Me and Willie McGee

What: Outfield

When: 1982-present

Where: St. Louis, Oakland,
San Francisco

Why Should I Know This Guy?:
Won the 1990 National League batting title, despite playing for the last month with the A's

Cris **If I Were a** Carpenter

What: Relief pitcher

When: 1988-present

Where: St. Louis, Florida, Texas

Why Should I Know This Guy?:
In six seasons has never balked

Chris **Mighty** Gwynn

What: Outfield

When: 1987-present

Where: Los Angeles, Kansas City

Why Should I Know This Guy?:
An inch taller and five pounds heavier than his brother – but still a singles hitter

Mark **Eve of Destruction** McGwire

What: First base

When: 1986-present

Where: Oakland

Why Should I Know This Guy?:

Has hit more home runs per at bat than any other active player

---

Lite Hits

Felix **Do You Know the Way to San** Jose

What: Outfield

When: 1988-present

Where: Oakland, St. Louis, Kansas City

Why Should I Know This Guy?:

May go down in history as the guy the Royals got in the Gregg Jefferies trade

ChrisNamesChrisNamesChrisNamesChrisNames

FELIX "DO YOU KNOW THE WAY TO SAN"JOSE

Matt **Forever** Young

What: Pitcher
When: 1983-present
Where: Seattle, Los Angeles, Oakland, Boston, Cleveland
Why Should I Know This Guy?: Juan Gonzalez has a .500 career batting average against him

Melido **Shuffle** Perez

What: Starting pitcher
When: 1987-present
Where: Kansas City, Chicago White Sox, New York Yankees
Why Should I Know This Guy?: Comes from a family of talented and enigmatic pitchers; has three brothers currently in minors

Todd **We Are the** Worrell

What: Relief pitcher

When: 1985-present

Where: St. Louis, Los Angeles

Why Should I Know This Guy?:

Cardinals closer, 1986-89; led National League with 36 saves in 1986

Steve Avery **and Ivory**

What: Starting pitcher

When: 1990-present

Where: Atlanta

Why Should I Know This Guy?:

Was MVP of 1991 National League playoffs

Marvin **Philadelphia** Freeman

What: Relief pitcher

When: 1986-present

Where: Philadelphia, Atlanta, Colorado

Why Should I Know This Guy?:

May be the second tallest player in the majors

Orlando **I Am** Merced

What: Outfield, first base

When: 1990-present

Where: Pittsburgh

Why Should I Know This Guy?:

Hit .313 in 1993

Greg **Life Is a** Cadaret

What: Pitcher

When: 1987-present

Where: Oakland, New York Yankees, Cincinnati, Kansas City, Toronto

Why Should I Know This Guy?:

Pitched a shutout for the Yankees in 1989 and again in 1992

Classic Rock

Mark Carreon **My Wayward Son**

What: Outfield

When: 1987-present

Where: New York Mets, Detroit, San Francisco

Why Should I Know This Guy?:

Hit .327 in 150 at bats for the Giants in 1993

Kirk **Devil with the Blue** Dressendorfer

What: Starting pitcher

When: 1991

Where: Oakland

Why Should I Know This Guy?:

In 34 innings in the majors, has given up seven unearned runs

Wally **Takin' Care of Business** Backman

What: Third base, second base

When: 1980-present

Where: New York Mets, Minnesota, Pittsburgh, Philadelphia, Seattle

Why Should I Know This Guy?: Hit .320 for the season and .333 in the World Series for the 1986 Mets

Ricky **Bad to the** Bones

What: Starting pitcher

When: 1991-present

Where: San Diego, Milwaukee

Why Should I Know This Guy?: Gave up 28 home runs for the Brewers in 1993

John **All in All It's Just Another Brick in the** VanderWal

What: First base, outfield

When: 1991-present

Where: Montreal, Colorado

Why Should I Know This Guy?: Has the longest nickname in this book

JOHN "ALL IN ALL IT'S JUST ANOTHER BRICK IN THE" VANDERWAL

Tim **Purple** Raines

What: Outfield

When: 1979-present

Where: Montreal, Chicago White Sox

Why Should I Know This Guy?:

Fourth on all-time stolen-base list

John **Teenage** Wetteland

What: Closer

When: 1989-present

Where: Los Angeles, Montreal

Why Should I Know This Guy?:

Had 43 saves and a 1.37 ERA for the Expos in 1993

Dave **Dead Skunk in the Middle of the** Rohde

What: Infield

When: 1990-present

Where: Houston, Cleveland, Pittsburgh

Why Should I Know This Guy?:

Traded by Astros along with Kenny Lofton to Indians for Willie Blair and Eddie Taubensee in 1991

He's known as the prince of stolen bases.

TIM "PURPLE" RAINES

ChrisNamesChrisNamesChrisNamesChrisNames

Oldies but Goodies

Bob **Old** MacDonald

What: Relief pitcher
When: 1990-present
Where: Toronto, Detroit, Houston
Why Should I Know This Guy?:
Sparky Anderson's closer for a couple of weeks in 1993; collected three saves

John **When Irish Eyes Are** Smiley

What: Starting pitcher
When: 1986-present
Where: Pittsburgh, Minnesota, Cincinnati
Why Should I Know This Guy?:
Proof of the perils of free-agentry; looking for a big comeback in 1994

Donnie **Blueberry** Hill

What: Infield

When: 1983-92

Where: Oakland, Chicago White Sox, California, Minnesota

Why Should I Know This Guy?:
Pitched one inning with Angels in 1990: no hits, no runs, one walk, one strikeout

Ron **Oh My** Darling

What: Starting pitcher

When: 1983-present

Where: New York Mets, Montreal, Oakland

Why Should I Know This Guy?:
Had five straight winning seasons with Mets, including 17 wins in 1988

Pedro **Harvest** Munoz

What: Outfield

When: 1990-present

Where: Minnesota

Why Should I Know This Guy?:
Only hit two of his 13 home runs for 1993 in the Metrodome

He can generate a pitch with that thing that few others can hit...

DWIGHT "**JOHNNY B.**" GOODEN

Dwight **Johnny B.** Gooden

What: Starting pitcher
When: 1984-present
Where: New York Mets
Why Should I Know This Guy?:
Has pitched 2,128 innings, and he still isn't 30 years old yet

Casey **Sixteen** Candaele

What: Infield, outfield
When: 1986-present
Where: Montreal, Houston, Cincinnati
Why Should I Know This Guy?:
His mother played women's professional baseball

Doug **Along Came** Jones

What: Closer
When: 1982-present
Where: Milwaukee, Cleveland, Houston, Philadelphia
Why Should I Know This Guy?:
Has allowed 355 fewer career walks than Mitch Williams

ChrisNamesChrisNamesChrisNamesChrisNames
I'll need an assist on this putout...
FLO
CASEY "SIXTEEN" CANDAELE

Kevin **Sing Along with** Mitchell

What: Outfielder

When: 1984-present

Where: New York Mets, San Diego, San Francisco, Seattle, Cincinnati

Why Should I Know This Guy?: Was National League MVP in 1989, when he had 47 home runs and 125 RBIs for the Giants

Instruments

Frank **Sweet Music** Viola

What: Starting pitcher

When: 1982-present

Where: Minnesota, New York Mets, Boston

Why Should I Know This Guy?: Led the American League with 24 wins for the Twins in 1988

ChrisNamesChrisNamesChrisNamesChrisNamesChrisNamesChrisNamesChrisNames

He's looking to hit a high pitch.

STEVE "ALTO" SAX

ChrisNamesChrisNamesChrisNamesChrisNamesChrisNamesChrisNamesChrisNames

ChrisNamesChrisNamesChrisNamesChrisNames

Steve **Alto** Sax

What: Outfield, second base

When: 1981-present

Where: Los Angeles, New York Yankees, Chicago White Sox, Oakland

Why Should I Know This Guy?: Used to compare well to Ryne Sandberg

8.
Sporty Names

Baseball

Todd **Which Hand Does He** Frohwirth

What: Relief pitcher
When: 1987-present
Where: Philadelphia, Baltimore, Boston
Why Should I Know This Guy?: Throws the ball submarine style

DENNIS "UPPER D-" ECKERSLEY

Jose **Game Winning** Uribe

What: Shortstop
When: 1984-present
Where: St. Louis, San Francisco, Houston
Why Should I Know This Guy?: Originally went by the name Jose Gonzalez

Dennis **Upper D-** Eckersley

What: Closer, used to be starter
When: 1975-present
Where: Cleveland, Boston, Chicago Cubs, Oakland
Why Should I Know This Guy?: In 1986, after 12 major-league seasons, he had three career saves; since then, he's had 272

Mike **Left** Felder

What: Left field
When: 1985-present
Where: Milwaukee, San Francisco, Seattle, Houston
Why Should I Know This Guy?: Stole 34 bases in 108 games with the Brewers in 1987

JIM GOTT **“THE WIN”** (LOSS, SAVE OR NO DECISION)

Bob **Intentional** Walk

What: Starting pitcher

When: 1980-93

Where: Philadelphia, Atlanta, Pittsburgh

Why Should I Know This Guy?:

Had 13 wins in 1993 to match career high for a season; now it's on to the broadcast booth

Jim Gott **the Win (Loss, Save, or No Decision)**

What: Relief pitcher

When: 1982-present

Where: Toronto, San Francisco, Pittsburgh, Los Angeles

Why Should I Know This Guy?:

Became Tommy Lasorda's closer in 1993, got 25 saves

Glenn **Mr. Outside** Davis

What: First base

When: 1984-present

Where: Houston, Baltimore

Why Should I Know This Guy?:

Cost the Orioles Steve Finley, Pete Harnisch, and Curt Schilling, but never healthy enough to help the Birds; in Royals organization in 1994

Basketball

Gene **Meadow** Larkin

What: Outfield, first base

When: 1987-present

Where: Minnesota

Why Should I Know This Guy?:

Replaced Lou Gehrig (half a century later) as Columbia University's first baseman

Rob **Double** Dibble

What: Closer

When: 1988-present

Where: Cincinnati

Why Should I Know This Guy?:

ERA of 6.48 in 1993 is more than twice as high as anything he'd previously recorded

---

Football

Vince **Four** Horsman

What: Relief pitcher

When: 1991-present

Where: Toronto, Oakland

Why Should I Know This Guy?:

Throws left, yet righties hit .212 against him in 1993, lefties .304

Scott **Goal Post** Kamieniecki

What: Pitcher

When: 1991-present

Where: New York Yankees

Why Should I Know This Guy?:

Popular name at the baseball spelling bee

In the Ring

Andres **the Giant** Galarraga

What: First base

When: 1985-present

Where: Montreal, St. Louis, Colorado

Why Should I Know This Guy?:

Hit .402 at Mile High Stadium in 1993

Gene **Full** Nelson

What: Relief pitcher

When: 1981-present

Where: New York Yankees, Seattle, Chicago White Sox, Oakland, Texas

Why Should I Know This Guy?:

Of 24 walks given up in 1993, 18 were to lefties; of 35 strikeouts, 30 were against righties

Lonnie **Liston** Smith
What: Outfield
When: 1978-present
Where: Philadelphia, St. Louis, Kansas City, Atlanta, Pittsburgh, Baltimore
Why Should I Know This Guy?: Has been to the World Series with four different teams

At the Racetrack

Kelly **Churchill** Downs
What: Pitcher
When: 1986-present
Where: San Francisco, Oakland
Why Should I Know This Guy?: Product of the Tony La Russa home for wayward pitchers

PETE HARNISCH
"RACING"

Pete Harnisch **Racing**

What: Starting pitcher

When: 1988-present

Where: Baltimore, Houston

Why Should I Know This Guy?:

Held opposing batters to a .214 average in 1993, the lowest in the National League

Etcetera

Franklin **Ticket** Stubbs

What: First base, outfield

When: 1984-92

Where: Los Angeles, Houston, Milwaukee

Why Should I Know This Guy?:

Had 102 career home runs; on July 25, 1990, played an entire game at first base for Astros without recording a putout

Dickie **Mara** Thon

What: Infield

When: 1979-93

Where: California, Houston, San Diego, Philadelphia, Texas, Milwaukee

Why Should I Know This Guy?: Overcame horrible beaning to the head in April 1984 that kept him out of baseball for a year

Bruce **Two Minutes for** Ruffin

What: Pitcher

When: 1986-present

Where: Philadelphia, Milwaukee, Colorado

Why Should I Know This Guy?: In 1993 had first winning record since his rookie season

9.
Literature

Albert **For Whom the** Belle **Tolls**

What: Outfield

When: 1989-present

Where: Cleveland

Why Should I Know This Guy?:

Had 23 stolen bases in 1993, 15 more than his previous season best

Dante **Inferno** Bichette

What: Outfield

When: 1988-present

Where: California, Milwaukee, Colorado

Why Should I Know This Guy?: Led American League outfielders with seven double plays in 1991

Mike **The Man Who Would Be** Kingery

What: Outfield

When: 1986-present

Where: Kansas City, Seattle, San Francisco, Oakland, Colorado

Why Should I Know This Guy?: Was back in the Royals farm system in 1993

Esteban **Bats in the** Beltre

What: Shortstop

When: 1991-present

Where: Chicago White Sox, Texas

Why Should I Know This Guy?:

Led American Association shortstops in total chances, 1990

David **War of the Worlds** Wells

What: Pitcher

When: 1987-present

Where: Toronto, Detroit

Why Should I Know This Guy?:

Performance in first half of 1993 made Toronto look foolish for letting him go; performance in second half didn't

Oscar Azocar **Named Desire**

What: Outfield

When: 1990-92

Where: New York Yankees, San Diego

Why Should I Know This Guy?:

Middle name is also Azocar

Andy **The Merchant of** Benes

What: Starting pitcher

When: 1989-present

Where: San Diego

Why Should I Know This Guy?:

Survived the 1993 season with the Padres

Terry **The Pit and the** Pendleton

What: Third base

When: 1984-present

Where: St. Louis, Atlanta

Why Should I Know This Guy?:

Revitalized career with the Braves in 1991 with batting title and league MVP

Mitch **The Devil and Daniel** Webster

What: Outfield

When: 1983-present

Where: Toronto, Montreal, Chicago Cubs, Cleveland, Pittsburgh, Los Angeles

Why Should I Know This Guy?:

Led the National League with 13 triples for the Expos in 1986

Now that's the way to whitewash a fence, kid...

CHUCK
"HUCKLEBERRY"
FINLEY

Chuck **Huckleberry** Finley

What: Starting pitcher

When: 1986-present

Where: California

Why Should I Know This Guy?:

Led the American League with 13 complete games in 1993

Terry **Grapes of Wrath** Steinbach

What: Catcher, first base

When: 1986-present

Where: Oakland

Why Should I Know This Guy?:

Another region-appropriate nickname

Tom **East of** Edens

What: Relief pitcher

When: 1987-present

Where: New York Mets, Milwaukee, Minnesota, Houston

Why Should I Know This Guy?:

Five years in the majors, has never balked

10. You Are What You Wear

Tux Cito Gaston

What: Outfield; manager

When: 1967-78; 1989-present

Where: Atlanta, San Diego, Pittsburgh; Toronto

Why Should I Know This Guy?: Had 29 home runs, 93 RBIs, and a .318 average with Padres in 1970; one of the few managers to win consecutive World Series

Joe **Flannel** Grahe

What: Relief pitcher

When: 1990-present

Where: California

Why Should I Know This Guy?:

Helped make Angels think they didn't need Bryan Harvey

Kirt **What Was That** Manwaring

What: Catcher

When: 1987-present

Where: San Francisco

Why Should I Know This Guy?:

His 432 at bats, 5 home runs, 49 RBIs, and .275 average in 1993 were all career bests

Jeff **See Through** Blauser

What: Shortstop

When: 1987-present

Where: Atlanta

Why Should I Know This Guy?:

Hit by pitches 13 times in 1993 to lead the National League

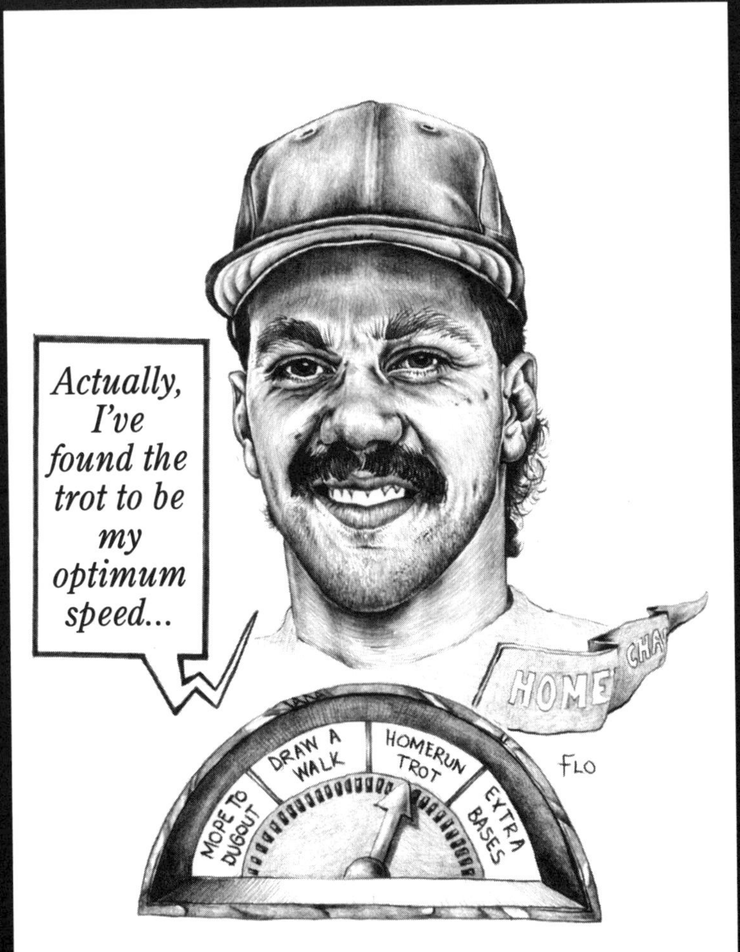

JUAN "SPEEDY" GONZALEZ

ChrisNamesChrisNamesChrisNamesChrisNames

11. Just For Kids

Cartoons

Juan **Speedy** Gonzalez

What: Outfield

When: 1989-present

Where: Texas

Why Should I Know This Guy?:

Career batting average for April is .302, for September and October is .232

ChrisNamesChrisNamesChrisNamesChrisNames

Al **What, Me Worry?** Newman

What: Infield

When: 1985-92

Where: Montreal, Minnesota, Texas

Why Should I Know This Guy?:

Hit one home run in 2,107 major-league at bats; signed as a scout for the Twins, 1993

Tom **Flash** Gordon

What: Pitcher

When: 1988-present

Where: Kansas City

Why Should I Know This Guy?:

Was once more highly regarded by the Royals than Kevin Appier

Felix **the Cat** Fermin

What: Shortstop

When: 1987-present

Where: Pittsburgh, Cleveland, Seattle

Why Should I Know This Guy?:

Laid down a league-leading 32 sacrifices for the Indians in 1989

He crushes all balls that come near the plate.

JEFF CONINE
"THE BARBARIAN"

Fred **Crime Dog** McGriff

What: First base

When: 1986-present

Where: Toronto, San Diego, Atlanta

Why Should I Know This Guy?:

Toronto acquired him from the Yankees as a minor league phenom for aging reliever Dale Murray

Jeff Conine **the Barbarian**

What: Outfield, first base

When: 1990-present

Where: Kansas City, Florida

Why Should I Know This Guy?:

Appeared in every game for the Marlins in 1993

School Days

Mike **Mathe-** Maddux

What: Relief pitcher

When: 1986-present

Where: Philadelphia, Los Angeles, San Diego, New York Mets

Why Should I Know This Guy?:

Four years older than brother Greg, but has pitched 1,208 fewer innings in the majors

MIKE "MATHE"
MADDUX

Mike **Pre-** Schooler

What: Relief pitcher

When: 1988-present

Where: Seattle, Texas

Why Should I Know This Guy?:

Had 33 saves as the Mariners closer in 1989

Floyd **Up the Down** Bannister

What: Starting pitcher

When: 1977-92

Where: Houston, Seattle, Chicago White Sox, Kansas City, California, Texas

Why Should I Know This Guy?:

Led American League with 209 strikeouts in 1982 for the Mariners; 3-2 with Yakult Swallows of Japan in 1990

Jim **Car** Poole

What: Relief pitcher

When: 1990-present

Where: Los Angeles, Texas, Baltimore

Why Should I Know This Guy?:

Career ERA of 2.37

ChrisNamesChrisNamesChrisNamesChrisNames

ChrisNamesChrisNamesChrisNamesChrisNamesChrisNamesChrisNamesChrisNamesChrisNames

He packs his trunk for every road trip.

JOHN ORTON

"HEARS A WHO"

ChrisNamesChrisNamesChrisNamesChrisNamesChrisNamesChrisNamesChrisNamesChrisNames

ChrisNamesChrisNamesChrisNamesChrisNames

Tell Me a Story

John Orton **Hears a Who**

What: Catcher
When: 1989-present
Where: California
Why Should I Know This Guy?:
Career batting average of .1995

Greg **Old Mother** Hibbard

What: Starting pitcher
When: 1989-present
Where: Chicago White Sox, Chicago Cubs, Seattle
Why Should I Know This Guy?:
Was the Cubs' best starter in 1993

Walt **Three Blind** Weiss

What: Shortstop
When: 1987-present
Where: Oakland, Florida, Colorado
Why Should I Know This Guy?:
Had career bests in at bats, hits, runs, RBIs, and average for the Marlins in 1993

Jose **Mother** Guzman

What: Starting pitcher

When: 1985-present

Where: Texas, Chicago Cubs

Why Should I Know This Guy?:

Has thrown 664 more innings than Juan Guzman, but has 10 fewer wild pitches

Gary Redus **a Bedtime Story**

What: Outfield

When: 1982-present

Where: Cincinnati, Philadelphia, Chicago White Sox, Pittsburgh, Texas

Why Should I Know This Guy?:

Thirteenth in career stolen bases among active players

Etcetera

Bert **Be Home** Blyleven

What: Starting pitcher

When: 1970-92

Where: Minnesota, Texas, Pittsburgh, Cleveland, California

Why Should I Know This Guy?:
Third most strikeouts in major-league history

Dave **Look, Ma, No** Hansen

What: Third base

When: 1990-present

Where: Los Angeles

Why Should I Know This Guy?:
One of baseball's best pinch hitters in 1993

12.
College Terms

Mike **Room and** Bordick

What: Shortstop

When: 1990-present

Where: Oakland

Why Should I Know This Guy?:

Fielding percentage of .982 was second best for regular shortstops in the American League in 1993

ChrisNamesChrisNamesChrisNamesChrisNamesChrisNamesChrisNamesChrisNames

ChrisNamesChrisNamesChrisNamesChrisNamesChrisNamesChrisNamesChrisNames

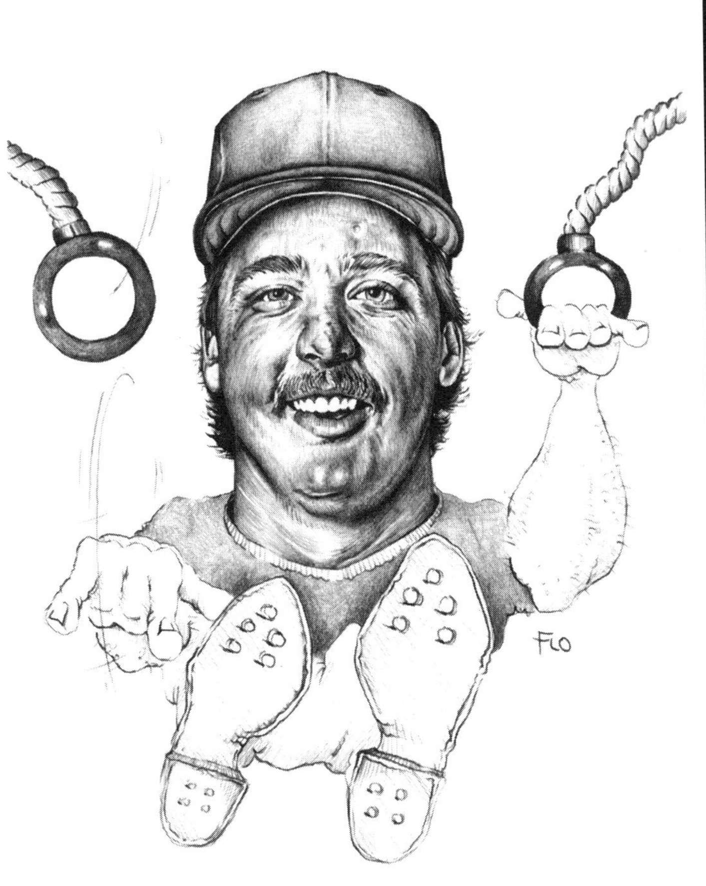

Another swing and a miss...

KEVIN "GOING" APPIER

ChrisNamesChrisNamesChrisNamesChrisNames

Jesse **Belly Up to the** Barfield

What: Outfield

When: 1981-present

Where: Toronto, New York Yankees, Houston

Why Should I Know This Guy?: Led American League with 40 home runs in 1986; spent 1993 season with Tokyo Yomiuri Giants of Japan

Kevin **Going** Appier

What: Starting pitcher

When: 1989-present

Where: Kansas City

Why Should I Know This Guy?: Some people think he's the best starter in the American League

13.
Out of the Air

Juan **Canadian** Guzman

What: Starting pitcher

When: 1991-present

Where: Toronto

Why Should I Know This Guy?:

Has a career record of 40-11

ChrisNamesChrisNamesChrisNamesChrisNames

Rob **Bomba** Deer

What: Outfield
When: 1984-93
Where: San Francisco, Milwaukee, Detroit, Boston
Why Should I Know This Guy?: With Hanshin Tigers of Japan in 1994

Gene Lamont **Cranston**

What: Catcher; manager
When: 1970-75; 1992-present
Where: Detroit; Chicago White Sox
Why Should I Know This Guy?: Spent eight years managing in the minors before the White Sox hired him

Tom **Lightning** Bolton

What: Pitcher
When: 1987-present
Where: Boston, Cincinnati, Detroit
Why Should I Know This Guy?: Has one save in 131 relief appearances

Jose **Flying** Melendez

What: Relief pitcher

When: 1990-present

Where: Seattle, San Diego, Boston

Why Should I Know This Guy?:

League batted .179 against him in 1993; may yet make deal for Phil Plantier a successful one for Bosox

14. Quotable

Chris **Bubbles, Bubbles,** Hoiles **and Troubles**

What: Catcher

When: 1989-present

Where: Baltimore

Why Should I Know This Guy?:

Average, home runs, and RBIs have increased each year

Randy **Bird in the Hand** Bush

What: DH, outfield

When: 1982-93

Where: Minnesota

Why Should I Know This Guy?:

Stole two bases in one inning in the 1987 League Championship Series, to tie a record

Rod Beck **Beck, Beck, Beck**

What: Closer

When: 1991-present

Where: San Francisco

Why Should I Know This Guy?:

Finished 71 of the 76 games in which he appeared in 1993

Rick **See Ya Later** Aguilera

What: Closer

When: 1985-present

Where: New York Mets, Minnesota

Why Should I Know This Guy?:

Has averaged 37 saves in four full seasons with Twins

Pat Mahomes **Where the Heart Is**

What: Pitcher

When: 1992-present

Where: Minnesota

Why Should I Know This Guy?:

Had 11 wins in 16 starts with Portland in 1993

Dave **No Man Is an** Eiland

What: Starting pitcher

When: 1988-present

Where: New York Yankees, San Diego

Why Should I Know This Guy?:

Threw his first wild pitch in 1993

Tony **Turn the Other** Perezchica

What: Infield

When: 1988-92

Where: San Francisco, Cleveland

Why Should I Know This Guy?:

Has 101 major-league at bats

ChrisNamesChrisNamesChrisNamesChrisNamesChrisNamesChrisNamesChrisNamesChrisNamesChrisNamesChrisNames

Murray! I said to grab a bat... not grab a bite!

EDDIE "EAT, DRINK, AND BE" MURRAY

ChrisNamesChrisNamesChrisNamesChrisNamesChrisNamesChrisNamesChrisNamesChrisNamesChrisNamesChrisNames

Jim **Home Thweet** Thome

What: Third base

When: 1991-present

Where: Cleveland

Why Should I Know This Guy?:

Led the International League in hitting in 1993

Tom **Goodnight, Sweet** Prince

What: Catcher

When: 1987-present

Where: Pittsburgh, Los Angeles

Why Should I Know This Guy?:

Has 402 at bats in seven seasons

Eddie **Eat, Drink and Be** Murray

What: First base

When: 1977-present

Where: Baltimore, Los Angeles, New York Mets, Cleveland

Why Should I Know This Guy?:

Is 180 hits away from 3,000 going into 1994 season

Juan **Play It Again** Samuel

What: Second base, outfield

When: 1983-present

Where: Philadelphia, New York Mets, Los Angeles, Kansas City, Cincinnati, Detroit

Why Should I Know This Guy?: Had 701 at bats, 72 stolen bases, and 168 strikeouts as a rookie for the Phillies

Sammy **Say It Ain't** Sosa

What: Outfield

When: 1989-present

Where: Texas, Chicago White Sox, Chicago Cubs

Why Should I Know This Guy?: Strong season in 1993 made the Cubs feel smart for trading George Bell to get him

Steve Lyons **and Tigers and Bears, Oh My**

What: Second base, elsewhere

When: 1985-present

Where: Boston, Chicago White Sox, Atlanta, Montreal

Why Should I Know This Guy?: Became a highlight-film star when he pulled down his pants at first base

Tony Gwynn **One for the Gipper**

What: Outfield

When: 1982-present

Where: San Diego

Why Should I Know This Guy?: Batting titles plus Gold Gloves equal a likely Hall of Famer

Rafael **Good Day at the Old** Belliard

What: Infield

When: 1982-present

Where: Pittsburgh, Atlanta

Why Should I Know This Guy?: One home run in 12 years

15.
Sounds Of Summer

Monty Fariss **Wheel**

What: Outfield

When: 1991-present

Where: Texas, Florida

Why Should I Know This Guy?:

Three of five major-league hits in 1993 were for extra bases

ChrisNamesChrisNamesChrisNamesChrisNamesChrisNamesChrisNamesChrisNamesChrisNames
ChrisNamesChrisNamesChrisNamesChrisNamesChrisNamesChrisNamesChrisNamesChrisNames
ChrisNamesChrisNamesChrisNamesChrisNames

Bill **Per** Spiers

What: Second base, shortstop

When: 1989-present

Where: Milwaukee

Why Should I Know This Guy?:

Spent most of 1992 on the disabled list, allowing Pat Listach to take over as Brewers shortstop and become Rookie of the Year; made transition to regular second baseman in 1993

Scott **Hay** Bailes

What: Pitcher

When: 1986-92

Where: Cleveland, California

Why Should I Know This Guy?:

Threw two shutouts for Indians in 1988

John **Charcoal** Burkett

What: Starting pitcher

When: 1987-present

Where: San Francisco

Why Should I Know This Guy?:

Had 22 wins in 1993 to tie for the league lead

JIM
"TWO SILHOUETTES
ON" DESHAIES

Steve **Poison** Avery

What: Starting pitcher

When: 1990-present

Where: Atlanta

Why Should I Know This Guy?:

Picked off 10 runners in 1993 — but his catcher only threw out 4 of 36 runners stealing against him

Jim **Two Silhouettes on** Deshaies

What: Starting pitcher

When: 1984-present

Where: New York Yankees, Houston, San Diego, Minnesota, San Francisco

Why Should I Know This Guy?:

Picked off 11 runners in 1993, to lead the majors

16. Legalese

Bernard **Innocent until Proven** Gilkey

What: Outfield

When: 1990-present

Where: St. Louis

Why Should I Know This Guy?: Career bests in average, home runs, runs, and RBIs in 1993

BERNARD
"INNOCENT UNTIL PROVEN" GILKEY

David **Chief** Justice

What: Outfield

When: 1989-present

Where: Atlanta

Why Should I Know This Guy?:

Has the same birthday as Steve Avery, April 14

John Habyan **Corpus**

What: Relief pitcher

When: 1985-present

Where: Baltimore, New York Yankees, Kansas City, St. Louis

Why Should I Know This Guy?:

Started 13 games for the Orioles in 1987 but none since

ChrisNamesChrisNamesChrisNamesChrisNames

17. Potpourri

Duane **Psycho** Ward

What: Closer

When: 1986-present

Where: Atlanta, Toronto

Why Should I Know This Guy?:

Pitched 30 fewer innings as Blue Jays closer in 1993 than he did as Tom Henke's setup man in 1992

Ken **Fix or Repair** Dayley

What: Relief pitcher

When: 1982-93

Where: Atlanta, St. Louis, Toronto

Why Should I Know This Guy?:
Appeared in 71 games for the Cardinals in 1989

Kevin Reimer **Reason**

What: DH, outfield

When: 1988-93

Where: Texas, Milwaukee

Why Should I Know This Guy?:
Picked by Rockies in expansion draft, but traded to Brewers before 1993 season; now in Japan

Clay **Ma** Parker

What: Pitcher

When: 1989-92

Where: New York Yankees, Detroit, Seattle

Why Should I Know This Guy?:
Led Northwest League with a 1.55 ERA in 1985

Don **Welcome** Mattingly

What: First base

When: 1982-present

Where: New York Yankees

Why Should I Know This Guy?:

More games at first base in Yankee Stadium than anyone but Gehrig

Bob **Yom** Kipper

What: Relief pitcher

When: 1985-92

Where: California, Pittsburgh, Minnesota

Why Should I Know This Guy?:

Threw for two innings in the 1991 National League Championship Series for the Pirates

ChrisNamesChrisNamesChrisNamesChrisNames

JACK ARMSTRONG
"THE ALL AMERICAN BOY"

Mark **Cigarette** Leiter

What: Pitcher

When: 1990-present

Where: New York Yankees, Detroit, California

Why Should I Know This Guy?: Broke into the majors three years after younger brother Al, but going into 1994 season had pitched 152 more innings

Jack Armstrong
The All-American Boy

What: Starting pitcher

When: 1988-present

Where: Cincinnati, Cleveland, Florida, Texas

Why Should I Know This Guy?: Has had double-digit losses for three different teams over the past three seasons

Scott **Rusty** Scudder

What: Starting pitcher

When: 1989-present

Where: Cincinnati, Cleveland, Pittsburgh

Why Should I Know This Guy?: Born on Valentine's Day

ChrisNamesChrisNamesChrisNamesChrisNames

ChrisNamesChrisNamesChrisNamesChrisNamesChrisNamesChrisNamesChrisNames

"Take three of these and call me in three innings."

JOE MAGRANE
"HEADACHE"

ChrisNamesChrisNamesChrisNamesChrisNamesChrisNamesChrisNamesChrisNames

ChrisNamesChrisNamesChrisNamesChrisNames

Chuck **Creme de la** Crim

What: Relief pitcher

When: 1987-present

Where: Milwaukee, California, Chicago Cubs, Seattle

Why Should I Know This Guy?: 1993 season was his first without a save

Hubie **Babbling** Brooks

What: Outfield, third base, shortstop

When: 1980-present

Where: New York Mets, Montreal, Los Angeles, California, Kansas City

Why Should I Know This Guy?: Was a college standout at Arizona State

Joe Magrane **Headache**

What: Starting pitcher

When: 1987-present

Where: St. Louis, California

Why Should I Know This Guy?: Picked off 10 runners in 1993 — but his catcher only threw out 3 of 25 runners stealing against him

Juan **Real** Agosto

What: Relief pitcher

When: 1981-present

Where: Chicago, Minnesota, Houston, St. Louis, Seattle

Why Should I Know This Guy?: Led the National League in appearances, 1990

Todd **Good Housekeeping** Zeile

What: Third base, catcher

When: 1989-present

Where: St. Louis

Why Should I Know This Guy?: Led the Cardinals with 103 RBIs in 1993

Don **On-** Slaught

What: Catcher

When: 1982-present

Where: Kansas City, Texas, New York Yankees, Pittsburgh

Why Should I Know This Guy?: Has hit .300 or better three out of four years with the Pirates

Ducks on the pond, Ivan...

IVAN **"BUBBLING"** CALDERON

David **Sili-** Cone

What: Starting pitcher

When: 1986-present

Where: Kansas City, New York Mets, Toronto

Why Should I Know This Guy?: Led the majors in strikeouts in 1992, without leading either league

Ivan **Bubbling** Calderon

What: Outfield, DH

When: 1984-present

Where: Seattle, Chicago White Sox, Montreal, Boston

Why Should I Know This Guy?: Stole 32 bases in 1990 and 31 in 1991; has never stolen more than 10 any other year

Bob **My Car** Ojeda

What: Starting pitcher
When: 1980-present
Where: Boston, New York Mets, Los Angeles, Cleveland, New York Yankees
Why Should I Know This Guy?: Has one career save, for the Red Sox in 1985

Art **And** Howe

What: Infield; manager
When: 1974-85; 1989-93
Where: Pittsburgh, Houston, St. Louis; Houston
Why Should I Know This Guy?: Fired by the Astros after managing them to their first winning season in four years in 1993

Ryan Bowen **Arrow**

What: Starting pitcher
When: 1991-present
Where: Houston, Florida
Why Should I Know This Guy?: Pitched his first shutout in 1993

Jeff **Brown Paper** Bagwell

What: First base

When: 1991-present

Where: Houston

Why Should I Know This Guy?:

Led the Astros in 1993 with a .320 average and 88 RBIs

Steve **Dorsal** Finley

What: Outfield

When: 1989-present

Where: Baltimore, Houston

Why Should I Know This Guy?:

Led the National League in triples with 13, 1993

Ryne **Carl** Sandberg

What: Second base

When: 1981-present

Where: Philadlephia, Chicago Cubs

Why Should I Know This Guy?:

Traded by Phillies along with Larry Bowa to Cubs for Ivan DeJesus, 1982; National League MVP just two years later

Ron **Extrava-** Gant

What: Outfield

When: 1987-present

Where: Atlanta

Why Should I Know This Guy?:

Has averaged 29 home runs and 34 stolen bases over the last four seasons for the Braves

Al Osuna **O Lata**

What: Relief pitcher

When: 1990-present

Where: Houston, Los Angeles

Why Should I Know This Guy?:

Has thrown three wild pitches every year in the majors

Eric **Ker-** Plunk

What: Relief pitcher

When: 1986-present

Where: Oakland, New York Yankees, Cleveland

Why Should I Know This Guy?:

Led the Indians with 15 saves in 1993